THE LIBRARY OF
AMERICAN
LIVES AND TIMES™

Ethan Allen

The Green Mountain Boys and Vermont's Path to Statehood

Emily Raabe

BPMS
Media Center

The Rosen Publishing Group's
PowerPlus Books™
New York

For Daniel, Rachel, Sara, and David, Vermonters;
and to our parents, who made it so

Published in 2002 by The Rosen Publishing Group, Inc.
29 East 21st Street, New York, NY 10010

First Edition

Editor's Note: All quotations have been reproduced as they appeared in the
letters and diaries from which they were borrowed. No correction was made
to the inconsistent spelling that was common in that time period.

Library of Congress Cataloging-in-Publication Data

Raabe, Emily.
Ethan Allen : the Green Mountain boys and Vermont's path to statehood /
by Emily Raabe.—1st ed.
    p. cm. — (The library of American lives and times)
Includes bibliographical references and index.
   ISBN 0–8239–5722–5 (lib. bdg.)
1. Allen, Ethan, 1738–1789—Juvenile literature. 2. Soldiers—United States—
Biography—Juvenile literature. 3. Vermont—History—To 1791—Juvenile
literature. 4. Vermont—Militia—Biography—Juvenile literature.
5. Vermont—History—Revolution, 1775–1783—Campaigns—Juvenile
literature. 6. United States—History—Revolution, 1775–1783—Campaigns—
Juvenile literature. [1. Allen, Ethan, 1738–1789. 2. Soldiers. 3. Vermont—
History—Revolution, 1775–1783. 4. United States—History—Revolution,
1775–1783.] I. Title. II. Series.
  E207.A4 R33 2002
  973.3'092—dc21

                                                            00–013023

Manufactured in the United States of America

CONTENTS

1. Who Was Ethan Allen?

Ethan Allen was on his way to the biggest party of his life. It was May 1778, and after two years and ten months as a prisoner of the British, Ethan was free and was returning to his home in the Independent Republic of Vermont. All of Vermont, it seemed, was coming to the town of Bennington to welcome home their hero. There would be cannons fired and muskets saluting him well into the night. There would be stories to tell, and as always when Ethan Allen was around, there would be plenty of merrymaking. Ethan was thin and tired from his years in captivity, but his spirits were high. He was coming home, at long last, to the place that he loved more than anywhere on Earth, the 9,600 square miles (24,864 sq km) that some called the Hampshire Grants, some called New York, and some called Vermont. Those who called it New York hated Ethan Allen and would have liked to see him

Because there were no portraits done of Ethan Allen during his lifetime, we do not know exactly what he looked like. Artists used descriptions of him to get his likeness down. This is a portrait of Ethan Allen by Junius Allen.

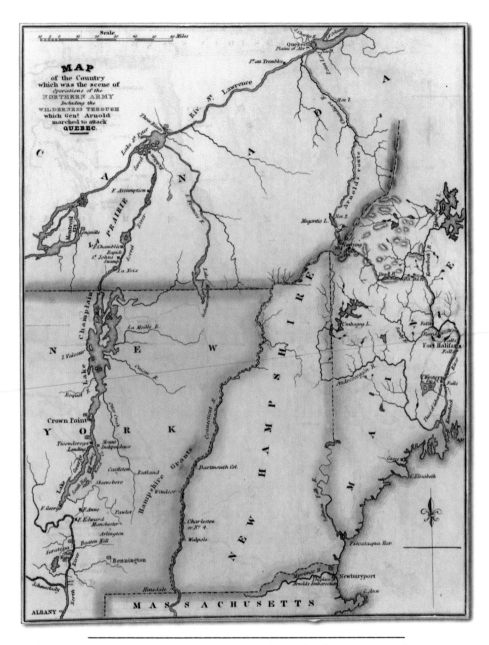

This is a map of the Hampshire Grants from the late 1770s. The Grants, highlighted in blue here, were bordered by Lake Champlain and New York to the west, and the Connecticut River and New Hampshire to the east. Canada was north, and Massachusetts was to the south. Covering 9,600 square miles of land, the Grants would be the source of years of conflict between New York and the Hampshire Grants settlers.

hang. Those who called it Vermont would follow Ethan to the ends of the Earth. Right now those fellow Vermonters were waiting for him at Stephen Fay's tavern in the town of Bennington.

On his way to Bennington, Ethan and his brother Ira stopped off in the town of Sunderland. There, a settler reported to them, a terrible tragedy was unfolding. The two young daughters of a settler named Eldad Taylor had wandered into the woods and been lost. Ethan must have been tired, but he immediately joined Ira and hundreds of other people searching the woods for the lost little girls. The searchers looked through the night and all the next day, and even the one after that. "We must call off the search," someone said. "There are cougars, bears, and wolves in those woods. It's cold and wild out there. The girls are surely dead." The exhausted men agreed. No child could survive two nights out in the wilderness alone. They would call off the search. Then Ethan leapt to his feet and jumped up on a stump to speak. As his voice rolled out over the woods of Vermont, the men gathered closer to listen to their hero. Ethan told them that he would not stop searching. The weather was getting warmer after the long winter, he reminded them, and the girls could still be alive out there, waiting to be rescued. He, Ethan Allen, would search alone, if that was what he had to do to find the children, but he was not giving up. Tears came to Ethan's eyes as he begged the men to keep on looking.

*One legend about
Ethan Allen claimed that he
could kill a deer by running after it
until it dropped dead from exhaustion.
Another one tells of the time that a giant
catamount leapt on Ethan's back one night as
he was hurrying through the woods. Ethan
wrapped his great hands around the cat's neck,
heaved it over his head to the ground,
and strangled it, all without ever
taking his hands from
the cat's throat.*

The tired men looked at one another and slowly, they began to get up off the fallen logs and the cold ground where they had collapsed in exhaustion. No one could refuse Ethan Allen, and no one did. The men went back to the woods, and the little girls were found a few hours later, cold, frightened, and hungry, but unharmed. Ethan Allen, hero of the Hampshire Grants, was home.

What is the story behind the Hampshire Grants, or the Grants, as the settlers who lived there called it? How did Ethan Allen and his followers come to create their own country in the middle of the American colonies? How did this tiny republic manage to fight off the British army, all of New York, and Congress for more than fourteen years, finally becoming the fourteenth state in the United States of America? The story of the Hampshire Grants, and of Vermont, is the story of an eight-year-long battle in which no one died, and of fourteen years of struggling to be free from New York. It is the story of a colony that became a country and then a state. It is the story of the Allen brothers and the Green Mountain Boys, and their battles with Yorkers, land-jobbers, thieves, and the entire British army over land. Most of all, it is the story of Ethan Allen, who was called by various people a soldier, hero, outlaw, traitor, philosopher, patriot, and the devil himself.

Who was Ethan Allen? To some he was a traitor. To others, he was the greatest hero of his time. He was a giant of a man, with a giant reputation: a man who could supposedly bite the heads off nails, and who could outdrink and outswear any man in the colonies. He got thrown out of two towns for fighting, and he wrote a book on religion that made every preacher in America angry. Ethan was a soldier, but he liked to think and write about philosophy and religion. In fact he liked to call himself "the philosopher." Ethan and his brothers and his friends governed Vermont for almost fourteen years, creating a republic with its own laws, courts, and army. Ethan had a terrible temper, and he had as many enemies as he did admirers. He was a complicated man who wrote books but who barely went to school. Ethan wrote a very famous book about his time as a British prisoner. At the beginning of the book, Allen wrote, "Ever since I arrived to a state of Manhood, and acquainted myself with the history of mankind, I have felt a sincere passion for Liberty." This educated-sounding fellow is the same man who was known to swear up and down to the devil, curse God, and promise his enemies that he would "tie you to this stump and skin you alive" if they didn't clear out of his way. The story of the Grants is the story of Ethan Allen, and it is a wild and unforgettable tale.

2. A Connecticut Troublemaker

One Sunday afternoon in 1764, in the town of Salisbury, Connecticut, Ethan Allen got himself inoculated against smallpox in front of the town church. His friend, Dr. Thomas Young, performed the inoculation. A small procedure, the smallpox inoculation was just a simple cut to put a bit of the virus into the patient's arm to protect him or her against the dreaded disease. However, this was no small thing in 1764. The church had a lot of power in those days, and the church forbade inoculations, seeing them as devil's work. Furthermore, Ethan was already known about town as a bit of the devil himself, swearing in the taverns, picking fights in the streets, and talking loudly about his disgust for organized religion. For Ethan to get the inoculation right in front of the church, and then to go boasting about it in the taverns, well, he must have been looking for trouble. As usual, he found it. A few years earlier, Ethan would have been whipped, branded, or even killed for acting against the church. By 1764, things were not quite so harsh in the colonies, and Ethan was

Thomas Young, in the above engraving, was one of the foremost proponents of what became known as Enlightenment philosophy. Young believed that individuals could understand anything in the world with the power of reason. A doctor, social activist, writer, and philosopher, Young was also one of Ethan Allen's closest friends.

brought instead to court. He was charged with breaking the peace and with blasphemy. Among other things, the court complaint claimed that when a Reverend Jonathan Stoddard threatened to bring Ethan to court for the smallpox inoculation, young Allen replied with a string of curses. These were serious words to throw about in those days. Ethan was fined by the court and was ordered to mend his ways. Not quite a year later, he was back in court, this time for fighting. The court record stated that Ethan and his brother Ira went out drinking with George Caldwell. During the night, Ethan and George got in a fight. According to Caldwell, Ethan "did in an. . . offensive manner with threatening words and angry looks strip himself even to his naked body" and attack him. Judge Hutchinson fined Ethan ten shillings and sent him home. A few weeks later, Ethan ran into George Caldwell and George's friend Robert Branthwaite. No one is sure who started it, but the three men got into an argument. Ethan punched Robert and then whacked George with a "club" (probably a stout branch) "in an angry and violent manner." When Robert tried to help George, Ethan hit him on the head with the club, as well. Ethan went his way after this bit of fighting, but later in the day was at it again. Seeing George on the street, he tore off his own shirt and "with his fist lifted up" shouted three times, "You lie, you dog," and swore to kill anyone who dared to fight him. Poor George Caldwell, who was by now

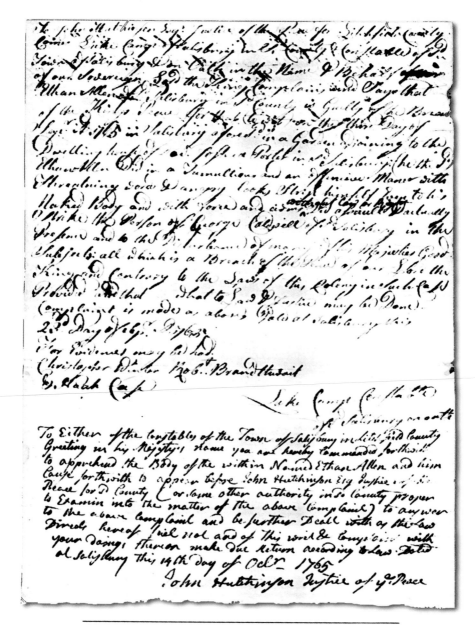

This letter is a formal complaint against Ethan Allen for his fight with George Caldwell in 1764. Luke Camp, the constable of Salisbury, Connecticut, wrote to John Hutchinson, justice of the peace, on September 23, 1765, showing that Ethan Allen struck George Caldwell, "which is a breach of peace." A writ was issued by Hutchinson to summon Ethan Allen to appear before him to answer the complaint on October 14, 1765.

probably bruised and exhausted by the fiery Allen boy, did not choose to fight him. Instead, it was back to court for Ethan, and another black mark against his already growing reputation in Connecticut as a troublemaker and fighter. This was Ethan Allen in 1764.

Ethan was born during a blizzard in the town of Litchfield, Connecticut. On January 21, 1738, with snow on the roof of the house and the wind howling in the wilderness outside, Joseph and Mary Baker Allen greeted their first child. Joseph named the boy Ethan, Hebrew for strength. Soon after Ethan was born, the Allens moved to Cornwall, Connecticut, where Ethan's brothers and sisters were born. Early on, Joseph Allen noticed that his oldest boy was something special. He was quick-minded and eager to learn. Joseph decided that Ethan should go to college at Yale. This was a huge sacrifice for a farming family to make, as it meant one less hand to help with the crops, but Joseph decided that it would be worth the hardship. He sent Ethan to Salisbury, a larger town than Cornwall. In Salisbury, Ethan studied with a reverend and prepared himself for Yale. Unfortunately, Joseph Allen died in 1755, at the age of forty-seven. Young Ethan was forced to return home to provide for his family. Instead of college, Ethan worked the family farm, and in 1762, he married Mary Brownson. Mary was nothing like Ethan. For one thing, she was deeply religious. She also was reported to have no sense of humor, and she was illiterate. It

This is the monument at the Allen Cemetery in Cornwall, Connecticut, where Ethan and his brothers were raised. The plaque on the monument reads: "To The Pioneers of Cornwall 1739–1763. Only Joseph Allen is known to lie here. Four of his sons Besides Ethan were at Ticonderoga." Joseph, Ethan's father, was one of the earliest settlers in Cornwall, arriving in 1740.

wasn't a good match for a brilliant young hothead like Ethan, and indeed the marriage was never very good. Ethan and Mary had three daughters together, but after 1770 he was rarely home.

Ethan, Mary, and their first daughter moved to Salisbury in 1763. Ethan was tired of farming, and the people in Salisbury had found iron ore in the hills there. Iron ore was melted in furnaces and used to make kettles, a good business in those times. Ethan and his brothers bought the rights to a hillside in

Ethan had five brothers and two sisters. His brother Heman was born in 1740; Lydia, in 1742; Heber, in 1743; Levi, in 1745; Lucy, in 1747; Zimri, in 1748; and Ira, in 1751. The Allens must have been uncommonly strong and healthy children, as every one of them survived to adulthood. This was almost unheard of in colonial times, when accidents and illnesses often killed people at very young ages. They were also a very close family, with a reputation for wild behavior and high spirits. Except for Lucy and Lydia, who moved away when they got married, all the Allens stayed close to one another and helped one another throughout their lives. Heman was the quiet one, the one who held the family together. Ira was the wily one, small but strong and clever, always hatching plans for the Allens. Levi was very smart too, although he would often disagree with his brothers, and Ethan was the firebrand, the one who could speak like a preacher and fight like a lion.

Photo credit: Norman Sills

This is a typical iron kettle from Salisbury, Connecticut. It was made during the same period that Ethan had his furnace in Salisbury. Items such as this one would have been used in the kitchen for food preparation. Furnaces allowed tools to be made from durable metal rather than wood as they had been in the past.

Salisbury and opened the Allen furnace. At the furnace, they melted iron ore and shaped it into different goods, like kettles, to be sold in the community.

Salisbury was where Ethan met Dr. Thomas Young, the doctor who inoculated him for smallpox in 1764. Thomas and Ethan became close friends, spending many hours together discussing philosophy and religion. They even began to write a book together, which Ethan would finish years later, after Thomas's death. The book was about religion and philosophy, and it got Ethan into a lot of trouble. For the present, Ethan was in enough trouble for fighting and using rude language in the taverns and streets of Salisbury. In 1765, Ethan sold the furnace and left Salisbury. Ethan moved his family to Northampton, where, in 1767, the town select-men held a meeting and voted to throw Allen out of their town. Ethan and his family moved back to Salisbury. In Salisbury, the Allens lived with Ethan's brother Heman. Heman had become a shopkeeper and was a steady, well-liked fellow. He was just the sort to keep Ethan in line, but no one could keep Ethan Allen in line for long.

Ethan and all the other Allens had a hard time during 1770. That year, Ethan's beloved sister Lydia grew sick. Ethan's brother Ira rode through the night to bring her medicine in Massachusetts, where she lived with her husband, but she still died. Ethan's mother died shortly after Lydia.

However, 1770 was also the year that changed Ethan's life forever. Early in 1770, Ethan and his brother Levi took a trip to explore some land that they had been hearing a lot about. This land was known as the New Hampshire Grants, or just plain Hampshire Grants. Although Ethan did not know it at the time, the New Hampshire Grants would become his home and his battleground for the rest of his life. In 1771, a Grant settler wrote in a letter that a certain Ethan Allen had moved to the Grants with "twelve or fifteen of the most blackguard fellows he can get." These "fellows," of course, were the rest of the Allen family. For better or for worse, by 1771 the Allens had arrived in the Grants, and the region would never be the same again.

3. The Hampshire Grants

The Hampshire Grants referred to a body of land that was only about 10,000 square miles (25,899.9 sq km). The state of Texas is almost thirty times this size. The Grants were bordered by Lake Champlain and New York to the west, and the Connecticut River and New Hampshire to the east. Canada was north, and the colony of Massachusetts was to the south.

Ever since the 1600s, many battles had been fought to claim the Grants territory. The Iroquois Nation of American Indians once controlled the area, but the Abenaki Indians defeated them and settled in the area sometime in the early 1600s. In 1609, the explorer Samuel de Champlain passed through on his way to Canada. He stopped to give his name to the great lake that the Abenaki called Petowbowk, and claimed the land for France. By 1763, after a series of battles between the Indians, the French,

This is an undated wood-cut of the French explorer, Samuel de Champlain.

Long before European settlers began to fight over property rights to
the Hampshire Grants, the area was largely populated by the Iroquois
Nation. Internal conflicts with other Native American tribes, as well as
battles with the new settlers, eventually forced the nation off the land.
Above is a depiction of an Iroquois warrior with bow and arrow.

and the British, the territory had come under British
control. At that time, Britain controlled most of North
America, including the thirteen American colonies on
the east coast.

Although the Grants were British territory and
were officially part of the colony of New York, very few
New Yorkers actually lived there. Thickly wooded and
home to many wild animals, the area did not present an
easy lifestyle for settlers. The winters were long, and
the summers were short and chilly. The soil, once the

The French and Indian War (1754–1763), was fought between the British and French over territorial rights in America. France and Britain were allied with various Native American tribes during the war. Above is a depiction of a battle during the conflict, entitled *Defeat of General Braddock in French and Indian War.*

trees were cleared, was stubborn and rocky. To make matters worse, many of the Native Americans living in the area had sided with the French in the wars and were not at all friendly to British settlers. For many years, the area stayed wild and unsettled. As the French and Indian War started to come to a close, though, settlers began to look to this new frontier as a possible home. As they did, a man named Benning Wentworth was ready for them. Benning Wentworth was the governor of the colony of New Hampshire.

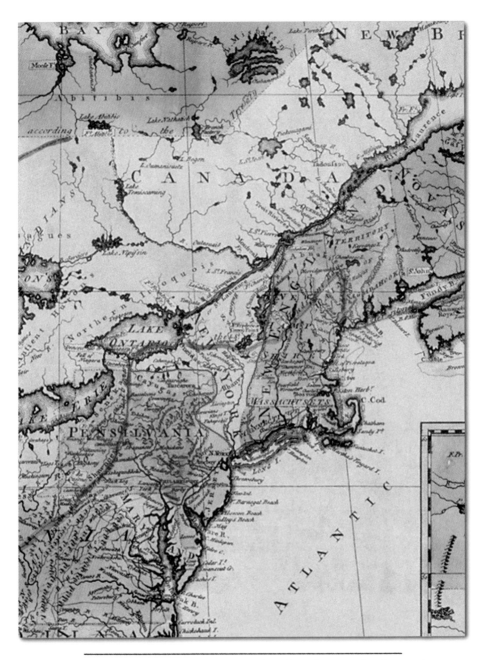

This is a 1755 map showing New England and several other colonies. New York is outlined in red, with New Hampshire colored green on its right. Massachusetts, colored yellow, is below New Hampshire. The confusing borders between New Hampshire and New York would eventually lead to the formation of an entirely new region.

This is a portrait of Cadwallader Colden by P. Purdon Graham after a portrait by Matthew Pratt. Colden became lieutenant governor of New York in 1761. He was one of the most learned men in the colonies. In 1727, he wrote *History of the Five Nations*, about the Iroquois, and a critique of Isaac Newton, *The Principles of Action in Matter* in 1751.

Benning was clever as well as greedy. After a few years in office, he realized that although the land west of the Connecticut River belonged to New York, New Yorkers were not really settling there. Benning saw an opportunity to make some money. He began to sell the land in parcels, called Hampshire Grants, to settlers. Benning sold the land very cheaply, and many people bought Hampshire Grants.

The acting governor of New York, Cadwallader Colden, figured out what Benning was up to and decided to put an end to it. Colden appealed to the British government to stop New Hampshire from selling New York land. In 1764, the British government passed a law known as the Royal Proclamation of 1764. The proclamation stated that all the land west of the Connecticut River belonged to New York. Having received Britain's answer, New York did nothing to enforce it. Benning Wentworth quickly realized that New York was not going to act on the Royal Proclamation. He continued to grant land west of the Connecticut River to new settlers, growing more and more wealthy from the sales. Governor Colden responded by regranting land, which means that he resold the very land that

Very few of the early Grants settlers came from New York. More commonly, they came from Massachusetts or Connecticut. There were also large numbers of settlers from Scotland in the Grants. These settlers read advertisements in the papers in Scotland for inexpensive land. Generally, the men from the families would travel to America first, clear the land, and build a house. Then they would go back to Scotland, get their families, and bring them back to the Grants.

Benning had already sold to settlers. This meant that land was being sold to two people at once! Things in the Grants were a mess. The settlers who owned Hampshire Grants were worried. Governor Colden was telling them that if they wanted to stay on their land, then they would have to pay the colony of New York. Most of the settlers didn't care if they were subjects of New York or New Hampshire, but they certainly did not want to pay twice for their land.

The Grants settlers sent a man named Sam Robinson to England to plead their case. Britain responded to the settlers' complaints by telling New York to do nothing about the situation until England could straighten it out. England, however, was far too busy trying to control her colonies in North America to think about a tiny patch of wilderness up near Canada. For the time being, England did nothing about the situation. New York, obeying England, also did nothing. Benning, on the other hand, kept selling his Grants, and the situation got more and more confusing.

One of the things that made the situation in the Grants confusing was that many people bought land there but did not actually live on it. These speculators, or "land-jobbers" as they were called, bought land only to sell it. Because of this, it was possible for a piece of land to be owned by two men at the same time, without either man knowing about the other man's ownership. A situation as muddled as the one in the Grants was a disaster waiting to happen. It was into this mess that a young man from Connecticut, named Ethan Allen, rode in 1770. Records show that "Ethan Allen, Yeoman" bought land in the town of Poultney on May 29, 1770, from a "Daniel Warner, Merchant" for four pounds. The next week he bought land in Castleton for six pounds. In March 1771, he sold his Castleton land for 24 pounds, for a profit of 18 pounds. Ethan Allen was in business.

From 1770 to 1771, Ethan moved his entire family to the Grants. Ira bought land in Poultney, and so did Heber. Ethan's cousin, Remember Baker, bought land in Bennington. Another cousin, Seth Warner, came to the Grants in 1771, as well. Both Remember and Seth would later join Ethan in the battle for the Grants, but for now the Allens were concerned merely with clearing land, building houses, and settling down. Their peace was not to last long. Things were about to heat up in the Grants, and the trouble would begin in Bennington.

4. Trouble in the Grants

In 1769 a man named Breakenridge was living and farming near the town of Bennington, on land purchased from Benning Wentworth. Although Breakenridge didn't know it, two New Yorkers, Major John Small and Reverend Michael Slaughter, also owned Breakenridge's land. In 1769, Small and Slaughter came up to the Grants to throw the settlers off the land. When farmer Breakenridge heard that they were coming, he and at least sixty settlers met them with rifles. When Small and Slaughter argued that they had the law of New York on their side, farmer Breakenridge gestured to the settlers at his back and said, "I hope you will not try to take advantage of us, for our people do not understand law." Small and Slaughter got the message and headed back to New York. There they went to the court to have Breakenridge and the other settlers thrown off the land. While Small and Slaughter were preparing their cases, the settlers in the Grants were having a meeting of their own. The settlers decided that they needed someone to represent them. They needed someone who was strong and fearless, someone who could argue well and who wouldn't back down. A man at the meeting suggested a young man named Ethan Allen. At that time, Ethan was living in Sheffield, just over the border in Massachusetts, but he spent most of his time in the Grants. Ethan had a reputation in the Grants as a fearless fighter, and one who would not back away from stirring up a little trouble with the New Yorkers, or Yorkers, as the Grantsmen called them. So it was decided. Ethan Allen would ride to Albany, the seat of government in New York, and have it out in court with the Yorkers. Ethan went to Albany, arriving on June 28, 1770. He hired a lawyer named Jared Ingersoll to represent the Grantsmen. Jared was a good lawyer, sharp and well-spoken, but it was clear from the start of the Albany trials that the Grantsmen didn't stand a chance. The lawyer for New York, James Duane, owned New York land titles. The judge on the case also owned New York land titles. At the beginning of the trial, James Duane stood up and said that Britain had granted the land to New York, not to New Hampshire. The judge, of course, agreed. It was over. The court had ruled for New York, and the Grantsmen were going to lose their land. Ethan

Next spread: This is a plan of the city of Albany from the year 1770, taken from the original survey by Robert Yates. Albany was and is the primary seat of political power in the state of New York. Ethan Allen would travel there many times attempting to negotiate for independence.

From the Original Survey by
Robt Yates.
In the Possession of the Honble G.Y. Lansing.

of the City of Albany. about the
Year 1770.

fort.

A.

A. Stuivesant Gate

rode back to his room at the local tavern that night, wondering what he would tell the men back home who were waiting for him to save their land.

That night at the tavern, Ethan had two visitors. They were the New York lawyers James Duane and John Kempe. The men had come with an offer for Ethan. If he would try to convince the Grantsmen to obey New York, then they would give Ethan money and a horse. "Remember," John Kempe told Ethan, "we have might on our side and you know that might often prevails against right." By this he meant that even though the Grantsmen probably deserved to stay on the land that they had worked so hard to clear, New York was stronger and was going to win the battle. Ethan rose to his feet so that he towered over the two other men. "Gentlemen," he told them, "the Gods of the hills are not the Gods of the valleys." Kempe and Duane looked at each other. What was this young giant talking about? Kempe asked him what he meant and Ethan replied, "If you will accompany me to the hill of Bennington the sense will be made clear." The New Yorkers had had enough. This sounded like a threat to them, and they had no intention of following this man back to his wild country where men ruled with muskets. They refused Ethan's offer, gave him money and a horse, and got out of there as fast as they could. Ethan rode his new horse back to the Grants, straight to Stephen Fay's Catamount Tavern in Bennington. There, over a bowl of

cider and rum, Ethan entertained the men by telling
them how he had taken money and a horse from the
New Yorkers. "But they wouldn't come for a visit," he
told the men at the tavern, who roared with laughter at
the cleverness of Ethan Allen. Ethan did eventually
give James Duane his horse back, riding all the way to
Albany to do it. The money went to the Grants, though,
never to be seen by James Duane again.

It was at the Catamount Tavern that the men of the
Grants decided to fight to protect their land. After lis-
tening to Ethan's story, they formed a militia, or army,
on the spot, pledging themselves to protect the Grants

Photo credit: Calvin Dart

This is a photograph of the Catamount Tavern owned
by Stephen Fay. This served as the central meeting
place for Ethan Allen and his Green Mountain Boys.

Stephen Fay's tavern was named after the catamount, a kind of mountain lion that once roamed all over the Green Mountains. Fierce, brave, and independent, the catamount was a good symbol for the Green Mountain Boys. The tavern, with its stuffed catamount mounted outside on a tall pole, became the headquarters for the Green Mountain Boys for the rest of Ethan Allen's life. Ethan and his Boys spent many hours there, drinking a wickedly strong drink called a stonewall which was a mix of rum and cider, and plotting tricks to play on the Yorkers.

from Yorkers. Ethan was voted in as their leader. They gave him the title of colonel commandant. Seth Warner was Ethan's chief field officer. Quiet and serious, Seth was an expert marksman. Some even said he could shoot an acorn out of a squirrel's mouth! Ethan's cousin Remember Baker, known for his easy grin and mop of unruly hair, became a captain of the group. Remember was strong and tireless, and like Ethan and Seth, he could travel in the wilderness for weeks without getting lost. Ethan's other captains were Robert Cochran, a fighting man who liked to call himself the Robin Hood of New England, and Peleg Sunderland, a tough old fighter from the French and Indian War who bred dogs up in the mountains. Heman, Levi, and Ira were named lieutenants, and Stephen Fay's son, Dr. Jonas Fay, became the group's doctor. At first, the men were simply known as the Bennington Mob. When Governor Colden heard about them, however, he said angrily that he would "drive that rag-tail mob back into the Green Mountains." Ethan knew a good name when he heard one, and so the Bennington Mob became the Green Mountain Boys. The Catamount Tavern became their headquarters, and the entire Grants territory became their land. Membership in the Green Mountain Boys was easy. All you had to do was stick a sprig of evergreen in your hat, and you were a Green Mountain Boy. For the next twenty years, the Green Mountain Boys ranged through the mountains and valleys of Vermont. They rode through the small towns of the Grants, calling for volunteers to join them on their "wolf hunts," as Ethan liked to call their battles with the Yorkers, and, later, with the British. The Green Mountain Boys became famous all over the world as Ethan Allen's strong, tough, and unstoppable band of merry men. It all started, however, in front of the fire at Stephen Fay's tavern.

5. Green Mountain Outlaws

In July 1771, the Yorkers were back at the Breakenridge farm. This time, the Green Mountain Boys were waiting for them. Henry Ten Eyck, the high sheriff of Albany, gathered 150 deputies and rode to the farm to get the land for New York once and for all. As the sheriff approached the house, he stopped in confusion. The farmhouse had been turned into a fort. The windows were boarded over, except for a small space just big enough to let the barrel of a musket poke through. There were muskets poking through these holes, too—at least twenty of them. In the field to the right of the house stood forty men, all armed. One of the sheriff's men pointed to a ridge that rose up behind the house. There on the ridge were what looked to be a hundred armed men, all moving about in readiness. In truth, there were only a few men on the ridge. The men had put their hats on the ends of their guns, and were moving them about so that they would look like many men. The trick worked. The Yorkers were very nervous. Farmer Breakenridge came out of the house to talk with the

Henry Ten Eyck was the sheriff of Albany in 1771. Of Dutch descent, his name, Ten Eyck, meant "the oak." Here is a family shield for the Ten Eyck family with several oak trees and leaves pictured on it.

sheriff, who angrily demanded that Breakenridge send his men home. "Well now," Breakenridge told the sheriff, smiling. "I don't own this land anymore. The town of Bennington does, and I guess the townspeople are just here to protect what is theirs." The sheriff was furious. He ordered his men to advance on the settlers. No one moved. The sheriff gave his order again. Only twenty of his men took a small step forward. The other New York men were afraid to do even that. There were just too many settlers with too many guns. The sheriff began to argue his case in a loud voice. "This land belongs to New York," he shouted. Very slowly, the men standing around the house and in the field next to the house raised their muskets so that they pointed straight at Sheriff Ten Eyck. The sheriff, faced with the steadfast Grantsmen, decided not to push his luck. He and his men left the land and went straight to Albany to complain to the governor about the rough Grantsmen.

No one was hurt, and not a shot was fired at the Breakenridge farm. This was the way the Green Mountain Boys liked to work. They talked big, acted tough, and usually chased away the New Yorkers without a fight. If tricks and talk didn't work, then they were not above giving the offender a taste of what they called the twigs of the wilderness, that is, a whipping with a beech switch. Most of the time, however, Ethan and his Green Mountain Boys used humor, tricks, and smooth talking to win their battles.

Later in 1771, a Dr. Sam Adams in Bennington began to speak out against the Green Mountain Boys. Dr. Adams was a Yorker who didn't care for the Green Mountain Boys, and he didn't care who knew it. In fact, Dr. Adams liked to boast that the Green Mountain Boys were a pack of rascals, and that he would shoot any man who dared to challenge him on the subject. Unfortunately for the doctor, word of his threats reached the ears of Ethan Allen. Ethan and the Boys snatched the doctor from his house and brought him to "court," that is, Stephen Fay's Catamount Tavern. There they held a swift trial and found the doctor guilty of being a public nuisance, which simply means that he was bothering people. Stephen Fay's tavern had an actual catamount out front, a stuffed one, mounted on a pole twenty feet high. The cat snarled west, in the direction of New York, as if to warn the New Yorkers to stay away. One of Ethan's Boys suggested whipping Dr. Adams, but Ethan had a better idea. Why not make the good doctor spend some time with the catamount? They tied Dr. Adams to a chair from the tavern and hoisted him up so that he hung in the chair at eye level with the snarling cat. Dr. Adams stayed up there for a few hours, long enough for all of the townspeople to come and take a look and laugh at the latest trick of those Green Mountain Boys. After a while, the Boys let the doctor down and sent him home, with an order to behave himself. Dr. Adams stayed out of trouble after that. That was how Ethan was. He had the

This is an illustration showing Dr. Sam Adams after he has
been tied to a chair and hoisted up to the stuffed catamount
on Stephen Fay's tavern. It was not an experience Adams would
soon forget. It was from stories like this that Ethan gained his
legendary status. This image was taken from the 1853 edition
of a book titled *History of Vermont,* by Zadock Thompson.

worst mouth in the Grants, but he didn't like to see
people get hurt. In the eight years before the American
Revolution began, not a single person died in the battle
between the Yorkers and the Grantsmen. Ethan pre-
ferred to use his cleverness to win his battles. He did like
his terrible reputation as a violent, dangerous man, however. Having a bad reputation made it easier to scare off
his enemies.

One time, Ethan captured two New York deputies and locked them in different rooms in the same house. During the night, Ethan hung two straw men outside of each window. In the morning, he told each deputy to look out his window. There the frightened men saw what they thought was the other deputy, swinging from a noose. "You're next," Ethan growled at each man. Then the men were allowed to escape, fleeing as fast as they could back to Albany, where they spread the tale of the cruelty of Ethan Allen. They spread the tale, that is, until the day the two men met in the street and realized that the clever colonel had tricked them. Ethan must have spent many nights in

On April 16, 1774, the Green Mountain Boys sent a letter to England about their struggles with New York. In the letter, the Boys explained their position of resistance, writing that "We are under Necessity of resisting, even unto Blood, every Person who may attempt to take us Felons or Rioters. . . it is not resisting Law, but only opposing Force by Force." This meant that if anyone went after the Green Mountain Boys, the Boys were going to fight back. They claimed that fighting back would not be against the law, because it would only be self-defense.

The catamount, or mountain lion, would become a kind of symbol for the Green Mountain Boys. It represented the Hampshire Grants' wildness in opposition to the more civilized image of New York. Above is a picture of a catamount statue based on the stuffed catamount from the tavern.

the Catamount Tavern laughing with his Boys over the foolishness of the New York deputies.

New York, however, was not laughing at the antics of Ethan and his Boys. In April 1771, Governor Tryon of New York declared Ethan, Robert Cochran, Remember Baker, and five other Green Mountain Boys outlaws. The governor put up signs advertising a reward for the capture of any of the men. When no one turned them in, he raised the reward, until it stood at 100 pounds. That was an enormous amount of money, and yet no one even

On May 19, 1774, Ethan found out that two Yorkers, Crean Bush and Samuel Wells, were telling Governor Clinton of New York that the Green Mountain Boys needed to be hanged to make peace in the Grants. Ethan wrote the two men a letter:

"But I have to Inform that the
Green Mountain Boys will Not Tamely
resign their necks to the halter to be
Hanged by Your Curst Fraternity of Land
Jockeys who would Better Adorn a halter
than we, therefore as You regard Your Own
Lives be Carefull Not to Invade ours for
what measure you Meat it shall be
Measured to You Again."

Do you understand what Ethan wrote in this letter? He wrote to Crean Bush and Samuel Wells that not only would the Green Mountain Boys not be hanged, but that Bush and Wells had better watch out, or the Green Mountain Boys would hang them! Ethan and Crean, especially, were enemies for their entire lives. Oddly enough, Ethan's beloved second wife, Fanny, was Crean's stepdaughter!

tried to turn over Ethan or his Boys and collect the reward. The New Yorkers were too afraid of the "mob" from the Green Mountains, especially their wild leader. No Grantsman, or woman, of course, would ever dream of turning in their beloved hero, no matter what the reward. Ethan responded to becoming an outlaw in his usual way: He made a joke of it. He and Remember got together and made their own sign. This one stated that the Green Mountain Boys were offering their own reward, for the capture of the two New York officials John Kempe and James Duane! The sign offered fifteen pounds for Duane, and ten for Kempe. Ethan certainly didn't have the money for the reward, but it made a great joke. Before long, settlers all over the Grants were reading Ethan's reward sign and laughing to themselves. "What in the world will he think of next?" they wondered. What no one yet knew was that an event was coming that would demand the attention of every person in the colonies, even in the Grants. There was a war on the horizon, and Ethan's next move would be nothing less than an attack on the army of the British Empire.

6. War with Great Britain

On April 19, 1775, American patriots attacked British soldiers in the towns of Lexington and Concord, both in Massachusetts. The battles were short but fierce, and suddenly, Britain and her American colonies were at war with one another. When Ethan heard the news about Lexington and Concord, he knew that the Green Mountain Boys had a new battle on their hands. In Ethan's mind, the Tories, as supporters of Britain were known, stood with New York as enemies of the Grants settlers. Anyone who would take the liberty of the Grants settlers was an enemy of Ethan's, and he didn't much care if he were Yorker or Tory. Ethan swiftly put out a call to his men to rally together and prepare for war. They came from all over the Grants and beyond. Heber Allen came from Poultney, a town in the northern Grants, ready to stand and fight with his brother. Ira Allen and Remember Baker came down from the wilderness of the Onion River area, even further north than Poultney. Zimri could not come to his brother's aid, as he had died earlier in the spring.

This is an engraving entitled *The Battle of Lexington*.
On April 19, 1775, the Battle of Lexington and Concord would
signal the official beginning of the Revolutionary War that would
lead to America's eventual independence from Great Britain.

On May 2, 1775, Heman arrived in Bennington, exhausted from riding through the night from Connecticut. Heman was bearing a message for Ethan. The Revolutionary Committee of Correspondence in Hartford had a request for Colonel Allen and his Boys: Could they please take Fort Ticonderoga, at once? Ethan was delighted. This was just the job for the Green Mountain Boys. Fort Ticonderoga stood on the western shore of Lake Champlain. Built by the French, it was taken by the British in 1763. Fort Ticonderoga was an extremely important fort for the British to have. From its position on the banks of the lake, they could easily get to Canada for more troops or weapons. They could also move quickly from Fort Ticonderoga into the heart of the colonies to attack them. For all of its importance, however, Fort Ticonderoga had been allowed to fall into disrepair. It was now held by only a handful of British soldiers. It was the perfect place to begin the war.

On May 7, Ethan and a crowd of about 130 Green Mountain Boys gathered in the town of Castleton to plan the attack on Fort Ticonderoga. On May 8, Ethan moved his men to Hand's Cove, opposite Fort Ticonderoga, where men from Connecticut and Massachusetts joined them. On May 9, they had an unwelcome guest. This guest was Benedict Arnold.

Ethan Allen and the Green Mountain Boys were instrumental in the capture of Fort Ticonderoga, which was an important and early victory in the Revolutionary War. Above is a photo by Lee Snider of the South Barracks at Fort Ticonderoga.

*Of the surviving Allen brothers,
Levi alone did not respond to Ethan's call
for help in taking Fort Ticonderoga.
Levi did not get along well with his brothers,
and he had not joined them when they moved
to the Grants. He stayed away from the battles
brewing in New England, moving south to
colonies that were more solidly Tory. Tories were
colonists who remained loyal to the king during the
revolution. They were also called loyalists.*

*Ethan later publicly denounced Levi as a Tory,
and had his land in the Grants taken from
him along with the other Tories. After the
Revolution, however, Levi and Ethan made peace,
and Levi moved back to Vermont. He went
into business with Ira, trading with Canada.
Levi spent most of the rest of his life in
northern Vermont and Quebec, Canada,
making deals between the Canadians
and the Vermonters.*

This is a portrait of Benedict Arnold. Arnold began the war a patriot but would later serve as a spy for the British and be tried for treason.

Benedict Arnold was a colonel in the Connecticut militia, and he wanted to take the fort himself. Wearing his fanciest bright blue uniform, and with a servant to brush any dirt off him, Arnold arrived on the morning of May 9 to take command of the troops. Benedict Arnold showed Ethan papers that he had gotten from the Massachusetts government. The papers stated that Colonel Arnold had the blessing of Congress to take Fort Ticonderoga. Ethan read the paper and then went outside to talk to his men. He explained to his men that the man in the fancy uniform was going to lead them, and that he, Ethan would not. The men listened, nodding. Then, one by one, they laid down their rifles in a pile in front of the baffled Colonel Arnold. Finally Arnold realized what they were saying. The Green Mountain Boys would fight under no one but their leader, and their leader was Ethan Allen. Arnold was furious, but there was nothing he could do about it. Ethan told Arnold he could come along, and could even march in front. "But stay out of the way," he warned Arnold, who could only sputter in anger. The

Ethan sent a young Green Mountain Boy named Gershom Beach to spread the word about the attack on Fort Ticonderoga to all the settlers in the Grants. "Tell them there is going to be a wolf hunt," Ethan told Beach. Gershom Beach went on foot through the towns in the Grants, covering more than 60 miles (96.6 km) in just 24 hours! Everywhere he went, Beach called out to the colonists to come join the Green Mountain Boys in their latest "wolf hunt." Ethan also sent a boy named Noah Phelps to Fort Ticonderoga. Noah pretended that he needed a haircut, and while the fort's barber cut Noah's hair, the young Green Mountain Boy counted soldiers. When he returned, he reported to Ethan that the fort was in bad repair, with not more than fifty Regulars guarding it.

Boys happily picked up their muskets again. The wolf hunt was back on.

In the early morning of May 10, Ethan and his troops rowed across the cove to Fort Ticonderoga. They didn't have enough boats, so only half of his men could join Ethan. The other half stayed in Hand's Cove. Arnold was marching in front with Ethan, as promised. The two men reached the doorway to the fort almost running, each one trying to get there first. In the end, it was Ethan who got there ahead of Arnold. The sentry fired at Ethan, but his gun misfired. Ethan Allen smacked the sentry with the flat of his sword and demanded to be taken to the commander of the fort. Meanwhile, to the dismay of the correct and careful

This is the Green Mountain Boys flag that Ethan and his men would have flown when they were going into battle.

Arnold, the Green Mountain Boys charged the fort, yelling and cheering in a state of happy confusion. Ethan Allen and his prisoner ran up the stairs, with Ethan pausing to bellow, "Come out of there, you damned British Rat!" A sleepy officer appeared, still holding his pants in one hand. When he asked in whose name this ungodly attack was taking place, Ethan roared back at him, "In the name of the Great Jehovah and the Continental Congress!" Jehovah was another name for God, but the British soldier had no idea what this Continental Congress was. The madman waving a sword in his face was convincing enough, however, and so Captain William Delaplace surrendered Fort Ticonderoga to the band of Americans without a single shot being fired.

Ethan and his Boys rounded up the rest of the British who were living in the fort and secured them. As soon as that was taken care of, Ethan sent one hundred men

Following Spread: This is a hand-colored engraving by Alonzo Chappel of Ethan Allen's capture of Fort Ticonderoga. Allen is shown as a commanding and forceful figure ordering the surrender of the confused British leader. Images like these would help to further Allen's reputation as a fearless soldier.

under Seth Warner and Levi Allen to capture the fort at Crown Point. Then, to celebrate their victory, the Green Mountain Boys removed 90 gallons (341 l) of rum from the fort. Legend has it that they opened it and had a marvelous party. The party went on well into the night and soon became an open house, with local people dropping by for a drink and to hear the story of the fabulous battle. The Boys also had a grand time teasing the horrified Colonel Arnold, poking his fancy hat with bayonets and even taking potshots at his bright blue coat. After four days, though, the rum was gone, and it was back to work for the Green Mountain Boys. Ethan wrote to Congress to

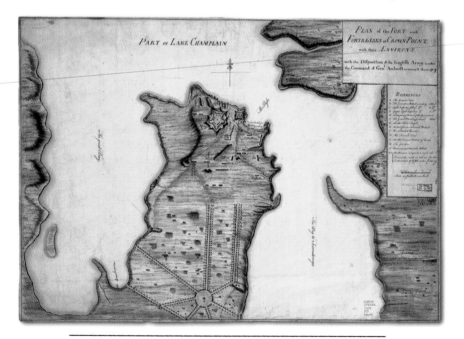

This is a 1759 plan of Crown Point. General Jeffrey Amherst built the fort in 1759, during the French and Indian War, after the French destroyed Fort St. Frédéric on the same site. The capture of the forts at Crown Point and St. Jean's assured American control of Lake Champlain, an important military victory.

announce the victory: "Gentlemen, I have to inform you with pleasure unfelt before, that on break of day of the tenth of May 1775 . . .we took the fortress of Ticonderoga by storm." A week later, the Americans had taken both Crown Point and St. Jean. This meant that the entire lake was under American control. The first attack of the Revolution was a huge success.

Although the Green Mountain Boys were delighted with their victory, Congress was a little nervous. Fort Ticonderoga was the first of the war's American attacks on British troops. Congress was still unsure whether they really wanted a war with Britain. Ethan rode all the way to Philadelphia to convince them that they did. His arguments must have worked, because by the end of his visit, Congress sent him back to the Grants with their permission to raise a Green Mountain regiment of the Revolutionary army. This was good news for Ethan for two reasons. First, he and the Boys got to fight the hated Tories. Second, and perhaps more important, by letting the Grants make their own regiment, Congress was recognizing them as their own territory. They would be a Grants regiment, rather than just part of the New York regiment. This pleased Ethan to no end. The Revolution had certainly not made him forget his true goal, which was independence from New York. The Grants would make their own army, and perhaps when the war was over, they could become their own state. It was a very happy Colonel Allen who rode back to Bennington to report the good news to the Grants settlers. However, bad news was soon to follow. The Grantsmen held a vote, and they did not choose Ethan to lead the new regiment. In fact, they did not choose him to lead anything at all. Seth Warner was made the colonel of the Green Mountain regiment. Ira was made a lieutenant of the new troops, and Heman and Heber were captains. Remember could no longer serve the Grants. Indians had killed him shortly after the battle at Fort Ticonderoga. The rest of Ethan's men, however, were voted into the new regiment. Only Ethan was left out. The men who voted on this new regiment were not the Green Mountain Boys who loved Ethan Allen. They were older men who feared Ethan's wildness and hated his blasphemous tongue. Seth Warner, by contrast, was sober and quiet. Ethan was hurt but took the vote with good grace. Titles were not important to Ethan. Freedom was, however, and he would continue to fight with the Grants for that. He pledged himself to Seth and offered his services as a scout in the northern areas of the Grants.

It was during his travels in the north that Ethan began to imagine a new conquest. This one was much bigger and more dangerous than Fort Ticonderoga. He wanted to attack the city of Montreal, in Canada. Montreal was controlled by the British, but Ethan wanted it, and he decided to take it.

7. Making a State

While scouting in Canada in 1775, Ethan met an American major named John Brown. Brown suggested that Ethan raise some men, and that together they could take Montreal for the Americans. Ethan loved the idea of more battles, more glory, and more fun. He couldn't wait. It was agreed that Ethan and about one hundred men would attack Montreal from the north. Brown and his men would move in from the south. By the end of the day, Montreal would fall, with luck, to the Americans. Unfortunately, luck was not with Ethan in September 1775. Ethan and his men attacked from the north, as planned, but Major Brown's troops never arrived. Fifty of Ethan's men ran away. The rest stayed to fight with him. The British outnumbered them, though, and in the end, Ethan and his remaining men surrendered to the British troops. Ethan and his men, now prisoners, were taken to the British general, a man named Robert Prescott. Prescott asked Ethan if he was the man who had taken Fort Ticonderoga. Ethan said proudly, "Sir, I am the very man." General Prescott flew

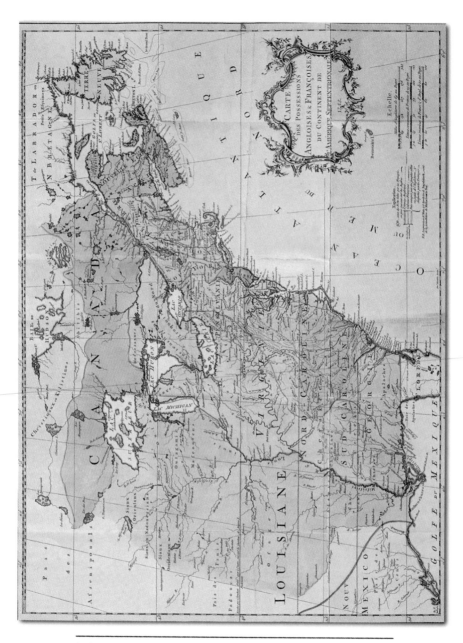

Most of the Revolutionary War would be fought in the American colonies, but some battles spilled into Canada, including Allen's ill-advised raid into Montreal. Above is a French map from 1755 depicting Canada, along with other territories in North America.

into a rage and began to curse at Ethan. The angry general said Ethan Allen should be caned or beaten. Ethan lost his temper. Leaping at Prescott, Ethan shook his fist under the man's nose and shouted, "By God, sir, you do well not to cane me, for I am not accustomed to it!" This made the general even angrier, although he did have the sense to back away from his wild prisoner. Then he told Ethan that all of his men would be killed. "Shoot them all," Prescott told his soldiers. The British soldiers hesitated. These prisoners were not even Americans. They were Canadian men whom Ethan had convinced to fight for the colonies. No one wanted to shoot anybody. Ethan saw his

While Ethan was a prisoner of the British army, he was kept in extra-strong irons because his captors were so afraid of him. One day, one of his captors was teasing the prisoner Ethan. In a fit of rage, Ethan bent down and twisted out the nail on his cuffs with his teeth. With a mighty effort, he yanked out the nail, spit it onto the floor, and lunged at the terrified British soldier who had insulted him. One of the other guards watching the scene said in astonishment, "Does he eat iron?"

moment. He leapt forward and ripped open his shirt. Pleading for his men's lives, he demanded that he, Ethan Allen, should be killed instead to spare the lives of his men. Now the situation was really confusing. The British soldiers couldn't just shoot Ethan while he stood there unarmed. Besides, as the leader of the troops, he was a prisoner of war and had to be treated decently. General Prescott gave up, realizing that he could not beat this irritating American. "I will not execute you now," he told Ethan, "but you shall grace a halter at Tyburn." Despite Prescott's threat to hang Ethan Allen later, Ethan had once again managed to escape death, at least for the moment. It was to be a long journey to freedom, however. Ethan would spend two years and ten months as a prisoner of the British. He would be passed from ship to ship, sailing from Canada to Ireland, Madeira, North Carolina, Halifax, and New York, while the British tried to figure out what to do with their bad-tempered prisoner. While Ethan was a prisoner, the Revolution raged on, and the battle for freedom in the Grants raged on, as well.

Between 1772 and 1777, the Grants sent at least seven letters to the still-forming American Congress, asking for their freedom from New York. Congress was too busy with the revolution to respond, however, and each time it merely asked the Grantsmen to wait until the war was finished and then the debate over the Grants could be sorted out. Heman Allen got on his

This 1776 portrait of General Robert Prescott is
an oval watercolor on ivory by John Bogle. The British
general was eager to execute Ethan Allen, but his
concern for British prisoners in American hands
kept him from acting on this desire.

VERMONT's
APPEAL
to the
CANDID and IMPARTIAL WORLD.

CONTAINING,

A fair STATING of the CLAIMS of
MASSACHUSETTS-BAY, NEW-HAMPSHIRE, AND
NEW-YORK.

THE RIGHT the STATE of VERMONT
HAS TO INDEPENDENCE.

WITH AN

ADDRESS TO THE HONORABLE AMERICAN
CONGRESS, AND THE INHABITANTS OF THE
THIRTEEN UNITED STATES.

BY STEPHEN R. BRADLEY, A.M.

The LORD hath called me from the Womb, from the Bowels
of my Mother hath he made mention of my Name.
And said unto me, thou art my Servant, O V ----- I in whom
I will be glorified.
And I will feed them that oppress thee with their own Flesh,
and they shall be drunken with their own Blood as with
sweet Wine, and all Flesh shall know that I the LORD am
thy Saviour and thy Redeemer, the Mighty One of Jacob. ISAIAH xlix.

HARTFORD:
Printed by HUDSON & GOODWIN.

Between 1772 and 1777, the Grants would send at least seven letters of appeal to Congress requesting freedom from New York. Such appeals would mirror America's own struggle for freedom from Great Britain. Above is an image of one such appeal that was probably written in late 1777, after the Grants had taken the name Vermont.

horse and rode up and down the Grants, convincing the people there that leaving New York was the right thing to do. Heman was not a speaker like Ethan. He had none of Ethan's easy charm and skill with language. He was steady, sure, and logical, though, and he worked tirelessly for the survival of the Grants. Ira was busy as well while Ethan was away. With the help of Jonas Fay and their friend Thomas Chittenden, Ira wrote petitions, letters, and articles defending the Grants's right to independence.

Ira and Heman Allen, Thomas Chittenden, Jonas Fay, and their supporters began their move toward independence in July 1776 in the town of Dorset. There, a convention of Grants towns wrote a document, known as the "Association." This association stated simply that the Grants were in full support of the American Revolution and would swear to "Defend, by arms, the United American States" from the British troops. Do you see the cleverness of this statement? Because only Grants towns signed the "Association," it had nothing to do with New York. This meant that the signers considered themselves separate from New York and able to act on their own. Writing the "Association" was a very smart move. It announced the Grants's independence. Things moved quickly after the "Association" of 1776. On January 15, 1777, representatives from towns across the Grants met in the town of Westminster for another convention. Ira and some

This page from the diary of Samuel Stevens was written on March 3, 1777. Stevens writes about how the Grantsmen have "formed themselves into a new state, called new Connecticut."

other people wrote a declaration of independence for New Connecticut, which was the name they agreed to call their new state. At the Westminster Convention, there was a formal vote for or against independence. At least three-fourths of the people voted "to be a new and separate state, for the future conduct themselves as such." So it was done. The Grants declared their independence as New Connecticut.

Jonas Fay, Thomas Chittenden, and Heman Allen left immediately for Philadelphia to give the declaration to Congress. The New York delegates in Congress were absolutely furious with the idea of this "New Connecticut." Who did these Grantsmen think they were? The Grants were part of New York, and that was final. Congress rejected the declaration for New Connecticut, and Heman, Jonas, and Thomas left for home, disappointed but not surprised. In a tavern on the way home, the three men met up with none other than Dr. Thomas Young, Ethan's old friend from his days in Salisbury. Dr. Young had two suggestions for the men from the Grants. Forget about Congress, he told them. Congress was too busy with war to help the new state. He told them to go their own way, make their own constitution, and wait. The other thing Dr. Young told them was that the name New Connecticut was already being used in an area of Pennsylvania. To be honest, he told them, it wasn't a very good name anyway. Dr. Young suggested Vermont, from the

French words for Green Mountains. Vermont sounded good to Heman, Tom, and Jonas. It was a strong name for a strong new state. The three men, convinced, left the tavern. The new state would be called Vermont, and Vermont would go it alone, without help or support from Congress or anyone else.

As soon as Heman Allen and the others returned to Bennington, they called a constitutional convention in the town of Windsor. In July, fifty delegates from thirty-one towns in the Grants met to discuss making a constitution for Vermont. As the delegates took their final votes on the new constitution, a horseman came

Above is Vermont's Great Seal, which was designed by Ira Allen in 1778. Images in the seal represent important aspects of Vermont as they were seen by settlers, including the wooded hills representing the Green Mountains. The tall pine in the center has fourteen branches, symbolizing that Vermont should be the fourteenth state in the Union.

The constitution that the fifty delegates drew up in 1777 for Vermont was the most liberal constitution in the entire Union. The Vermonters believed in democracy for all, and they were determined that their constitution would reflect that. The Vermont constitution put the power in the people's hands. The state would be governed by town meetings, rather than by just a few leaders. Vermont's constitution was also the only constitution in the Union at that time to outlaw slavery. Any slave who crossed the border into Vermont instantly would be free, and he or she could not be forced to return to his or her master in another state. Vermont had different laws for voting, as well. They created something called "universal manhood suffrage." This simply meant that any man over 21 who had lived in Vermont for a year could vote, whether or not he owned any property. Notice the word "manhood." Unfortunately, women did not get to vote in Vermont until 1920, when Congress passed the Nineteenth Amendment, giving women the right to vote. In the 1700s, however, not even all men were allowed to vote. Most states at that time only let rich land-owners vote. In Vermont, if you arrived, you were welcome. If you wanted to live there, then you could, and you had all the rights of any other Vermonter.

clattering into the yard. "Fort Ticonderoga has fallen," he cried. "The British Regulars are coming!" The fifty delegates quickly signed the constitution, put an emergency government into power, called a council of safety, grabbed their guns, and ran for their horses. As far as they were concerned, Vermont was officially an independent republic, and now it was time to get back to the war against the British.

8. Ethan Returns

Ethan Allen was a prisoner of the British from 1775 to 1778. He was perhaps the most famous prisoner that the British held, and they were not sure what to do with him. They couldn't hang him, because then the Americans would hang British prisoners of war in response. Ethan ended up on British ships, kept a prisoner down in the hold for months on end. Although he and his men were treated horribly, Ethan held onto his spirit, not to mention his legendary temper. When he arrived in Falmouth, England, to be held at Pendennis Castle, the streets were so jammed with people who had turned out to see the wild man from America that Ethan's guards had to fight their way through the crowds with their swords drawn. People came from all over England to meet the prisoner, who, rumors said, chewed iron for breakfast and drank a gallon of rum every day. Ethan had a wonderful time talking to his visitors. He argued with them about religion and freedom, and he informed them that America would surely triumph and be a free country

This engraving by Henry Winkles, from an 1851 encyclopedia (*Iconographic Encyclopedia, Vol. III*), shows sailors in irons. Ethan was shackled in the hold of a ship called *Gespé*, as well as several others, during his captivity, and was often unable to lie down or move about. Prescott wanted to make him as uncomfortable as possible.

soon. After Pendennis, Ethan was taken by ship to Cork, Ireland, where the local people boarded the ship to bring him gifts. Ethan later wrote that the kind people of Cork brought him beautiful clothes and "wine of the best sort, old spirits...brown sugar, coffee, tea, and chocolate, with a large round of pickled beef, and a number of fat turkies." Ethan's furious guards took his food, but they were too late for the rest: He had already managed to hide the wine and the spirits. Ethan finally landed in New York City in October

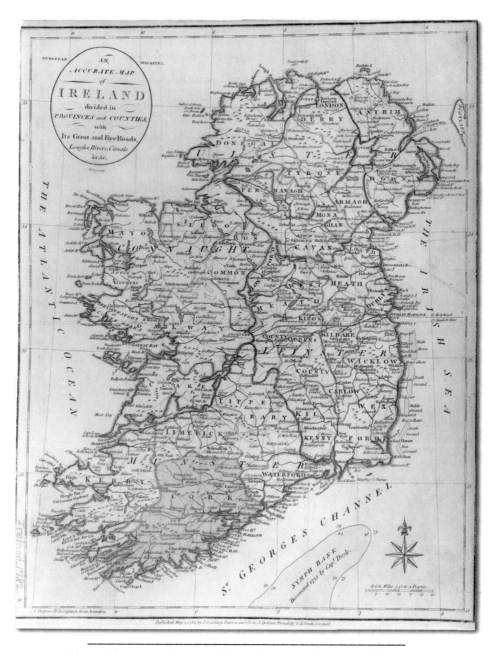

Ethan Allen was kept in Cork, Ireland, for part of the time
that he was held as a prisoner of war. Many people in Ireland
also wanted independence from Britain, and they sympathized
with America and Ethan Allen. Above is a map of Ireland
from 1782. County Cork has been highlighted in blue.

This is the manuscript of George Washington's May 1778 letter to Congress describing Ethan Allen. Washington was quite impressed by his meeting with Allen, writing of him: "His long captivity and sufferings have only served to increase, if possible, his enthusiastic zeal."

1776. New York was controlled by the British, and Ethan was held there until May 1778, when he was finally released.

The entire time that Ethan was a prisoner, Ira and Levi worked hard to get him released. Levi especially used his money and influence with the British to try and gain freedom for his older brother. They may not have agreed on politics, but they were Allens, and Allens took care of one another. It was Levi who finally organized Ethan's release. Ethan was traded for a British prisoner of war, Colonel Archibald Campbell. On May 8, 1778, Ethan Allen was escorted to the camp of General George Washington. The American general had heard many stories about the hero of the Grants, and he wanted to meet the legend in person. Washington was impressed. Ethan's "fortitude and firmness seem to have placed him out of the reach of misfortune," General Washington wrote to Congress after the meeting. "There is an original something in him that commands attention." General Washington sent Ethan back to Vermont to carry on the fight from his home. He went gladly, delighted to be headed home at long last.

The Vermont that Ethan was returning to was very different from the Grants that he had left. It was now an independent republic, existing against the orders of Congress. In 1777, Congress had ordered Vermont to "cease to exist," an order that Vermont ignored. This meant that Vermont now stood against New York, Great Britain, and the entire Congress of the United States. Things closer to home had changed, as well. Ethan's only son died of smallpox while Ethan was in prison, and Heman, the strength of the family, had died in his old home in Salisbury only a week before Ethan's release. Ethan was returning to some hard

A

NARRATIVE

O F

Colonel Ethan Allen's

CAPTIVITY,

From the Time of his being taken by the British, near Montreal, on
the 25th Day of September, in the Year 1775, to the Time of
his Exchange, on the 6th Day of May, 1778:

C O N T A I N I N G,

His VOYAGES AND TRAVELS,

With the most remarkable Occurrences respecting himself, and many
other Continental Prisoners of different Ranks and Characters,
which fell under his Observation, in the Course of the same;
particularly the Destruction of the Prisoners at New York, by
General Sir William Howe, in the Years 1776 and 1777.

Interspersed with some POLITICAL OBSERVATIONS.

Written by himself, and now published for the Information of the Curious in all Nations.

When God from Chaos gave this World to be,
Man then he form'd, and form'd him TO BE FREE.
American Independence, a Poem, by FRANEAU.

P H I L A D E L P H I A : PRINTED,
B O S T O N : Re-printed
BY DRAPER AND FOLSOM, AT THEIR *Printing*
Office, AT THE CORNER OF *Winter-Street.*
M.DEC,LXXXX.

This is the title page of Ethan Allen's 1790 book about his two-
and-a-half years as a prisoner of the British. As he said,
it was written "for the information of the Curious in all Nations."

times. But he was also returning as a hero, and the entire state was ready and waiting to welcome home their hero.

One of the first things that Ethan did when he got home was to sit down and write a book. The title of the book was *A Narrative of Colonel Ethan Allen's Captivity*. Ethan's book told the story of his capture by the British, and of his two-and-a-half years as a prisoner. The book was a huge success. People all across the country read about the evil behavior of the British jailers, and the bravery and honor of the American prisoners, especially Ethan Allen. In the book, Ethan was careful to mix up the dreaded Tories with Yorkers, making them both evil. In this way, he made Vermont's right to be independent from New York the same thing as America's right to be independent from Britain. Both America and Vermont had a long way to go to gain their independence, however.

Heman, Zimri, and Lydia Allen were dead. Levi Allen was a Tory. That left Ira and Ethan Allen and their supporters to govern Vermont. Ethan's old friend Thomas Chittenden was the governor for Vermont. Ira was the treasurer, which meant that he controlled all the state's money. Almost all of the judges and council members were friends of the Allens. Anyone who threatened the state, even other Vermonters, had to answer to the Green Mountain Boys, who answered to Ethan. Ethan alone did not hold any official position.

This 1873 portrait of Thomas Chittenden was etched by H. B. Hall. Chittenden lived from 1730 to 1797. He was elected governor of the republic of Vermont at the Windsor Convention in 1777. He was still governor when Vermont was accepted into the Union in 1791 and remained in office until his death in 1797.

He didn't need to. He was the unofficial spokesman for Vermont, called upon to settle disputes, rally support, or sort out disturbances. His main duty during the late 1700s was to act as a negotiator. Ethan negotiated with Congress, with the New Yorkers, and even with the British in his efforts to win statehood for Vermont

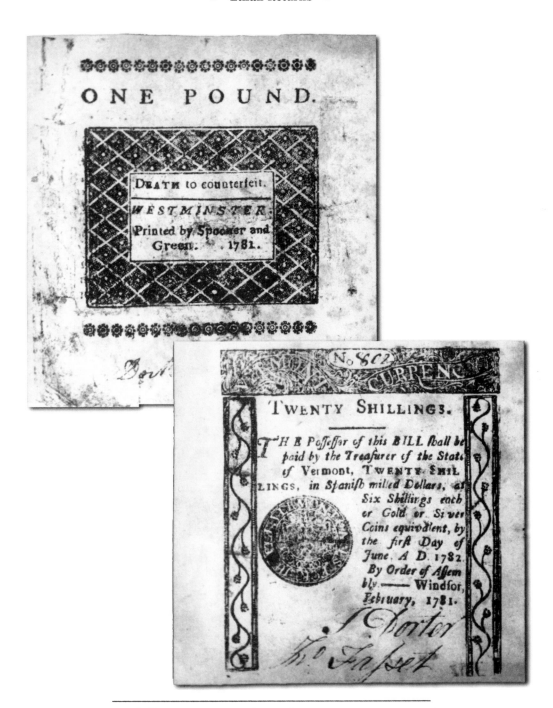

As a way of illustrating its independence, Vermont set up its own
system of courts, political institutions, and minted money.
Above are two examples of Vermont bills from 1781.

In 1778, sixteen towns in New Hampshire decided that they wanted to be Vermonters, too. They asked Vermont to annex them, which means to take them over and make them part of the state of Vermont. Naturally, Congress was angry at Vermont for doing this, but the Vermonters knew what they were doing. They offered to send the towns back to New Hampshire if Congress would make them a state. The deal was struck, and the towns went back to New Hampshire. Then, Congress not only backed out on the deal but again issued an order telling Vermont to cease to exist immediately. The Vermonters were furious. Thomas Chittenden wrote a letter to Congress explaining Vermont's position. "We are in the fullest sense as unwilling to be under the jurisdiction of New-York as we can conceive America would be to revert back under the power of great Britain," he wrote in the letter. Tom's language was a bit complicated, but his meaning was clear. If America was to be free from the British, then Vermont would be free from New York.

once and for all. Congress held firm, however. According to them, Vermont was a part of New York, and that was final. The Vermonters began to despair of ever becoming a state.

Late in 1780, Ethan received a letter. The letter was from a Tory commander, and it offered a deal to Ethan and Vermont. If Vermont would join Great Britain in the war, then they would allow the tiny republic to keep its government and freedom, although technically it would still be under British law. Ethan quickly showed the letter to Ira and Tom. The three of them knew that they could use this British interest to help their fight for freedom. Ethan knew a British spy named John Williams. During a conversation with John, Ethan let him know that he would "run on the mountains and live on mouse meat" before he would give in to New York or to Congress. Ethan knew that John Williams would repeat his words to the British command. Sure enough, John Williams did report the conversation to the British. This made the British feel that Colonel Allen might come to their side to escape New York's power. At the same time, Ethan wrote a letter to George Washington promising that Vermont would never go over to the side of the British. Clever Ethan had done it again. The British, thinking that they had won Ethan Allen and Vermont, would not attack Vermont. Congress, eager to hold onto Vermont, also would not attack Vermont. This meant that

Vermont could go quietly about her business, an independent republic ringed by enemies and yet attacked
by no one. For the moment, Ethan Allen had won
peace for Vermont. Now all he needed was permission
from Congress for Vermont to become a state.

9. The Independent Republic of Vermont

Although the problems with Congress and the British were under control for the time being, Ethan and the Green Mountain Boys still had their hands full keeping order in Vermont. There were still a few pockets of Yorkers living in Vermont, and some of them were causing trouble. Laws in Vermont were very strict. Anyone acting against Vermont could be whipped, branded, or have his or her ear nailed to a post. Anyone who was either a Yorker or a Tory could be thrown off his land, and his house could be burned to the ground. In fact, any Yorker or Tory who did not take an oath of allegiance to Vermont was thrown out of the state forever. The young government paid its bills with the money earned selling these lands once the Yorkers and Tories were banished. Ira, Ethan's clever brother, came up with this plan early in the Revolutionary War. Vermont made so much money selling Yorker and Tory land that although all of the other states had huge debts after the war, Vermont alone had none.

Although these harsh laws meant that most Yorkers and Tories either left Vermont or joined the Vermonters, there were still a few places where people supported New York rule. The town of Guilford was one of those places. Guilford had a New York charter, and the townspeople considered themselves New Yorkers. They held their own elections and had their own sheriff, a New Yorker named Timothy Phelps. Phelps was known as a violent man, who had once attacked a Vermont official with a pitchfork. He liked to boast that he wasn't afraid of the Green Mountain Boys, and that he would whip any one of them who came to his town. In the fall of 1782, Ethan got word that the town of Guilford was causing trouble in Vermont. Ethan knew that the only way Vermont could survive was by all the towns working together. If Guilford stayed with New York, it could destroy the future of Vermont. Besides, Ethan decided, the Green Mountain Boys couldn't allow a Yorker sheriff to attack Vermonters with a pitchfork. Timothy Phelps needed to be taught a lesson. Ethan saddled up his black horse, put on his old uniform, and began to gather the Green Mountain Boys for one more wolf hunt. Ethan sent Ira and some of the men ahead to Guilford as a scouting party. The people of Guilford knew they were coming, however, and they ambushed Ira and

Opposite Page: This is a map of the state of Vermont. Guilford, highlighted in purple, had a New York charter and was not interested in becoming part of a new state. Ethan went to the town in 1782 to make sure its people changed their minds.

C A N A D A

MAP OF THE
STATE OF VERMONT,

SCALE OF MILES

STATE OF NEW HAMPSHIRE

LAKE CHAMPLAIN

STATE OF MASSACHUSETTS

EXPLANATION
— County Divisions
— Contested Lines
— Publick Roads
Meeting Houses
Forts

Drawn in the offices of the State of Vermont,
Department of Highways, 1941, abridged from
a copy of the map engraved and printed for
William Blodget by Amos Doolittle, 1789
By special permission of The American
Antiquarian Society

his men outside town. The Green Mountain Boys retreated and went back to tell their general what had happened. Ethan flew into a rage. Leaping on his horse, he rode straight into the center of Guilford, with a hundred men on horses at his back. Ethan stopped in the center of town and shouted in his loudest voice, "I, Ethan Allen, do declare that I will give no quarter to the man, woman, or child who shall oppose me, and unless the inhabitants of Guilford peacefully submit to the authority of Vermont, I swear I will lay it as desolate as Sodom and Gomorrah, by God!" Sodom and Gomorrah, as the Guilford residents well knew, were two towns in the Bible that were destroyed by God. The townspeople knew that Ethan and his men had whipped Yorkers and burned their houses in the past. They believed his terrible threats and fled to their homes in terror. Ethan wasn't finished yet. He called for his men to bring him the Yorker sheriff, Timothy Phelps. Phelps was dragged before Ethan, who still sat on his great, black horse. The furious Yorker sheriff cursed Ethan, Vermont, and all the Green Mountain Boys until he wore himself out and stopped to catch his breath. Then Ethan leaned down over Sheriff Phelps, and with one swift arc of his huge sword, he cut the man's hat neatly off his head. "Take this damned rascal out of the way," he said to his men. Ethan rode directly from Guilford to Brattleboro, another Yorker town that had been causing trouble for Vermont. He and his men rounded up the Yorkers in the town. Ethan sent the Yorkers from Guilford and Brattleboro to stand trial in Westminster as traitors to Vermont. Most of the Yorkers got off lightly, with fines, and were offered places in Vermont if they would take the pledge of allegiance to the state. Almost all of them chose to take the pledge and to remain in Vermont as Vermonters, New Yorkers no more. A few of the men, however, the loudmouthed Phelps in particular, were thrown out of Vermont forever, their land taken away and their houses burned. "You have called on your God Clinton," Ethan sneered at the Yorkers, meaning Governor Clinton of New York. "Now go call on your God Congress, and they will answer you as Clinton has done." With that, Ethan Allen threw the men out of Vermont and sent them back to Albany to complain, once again, to Governor Clinton and to Congress. As Ethan had promised, neither Governor Clinton nor Congress did anything about the battles at Guilford and Brattleboro. The Green Mountain Boys were just too strong. It was clear to everyone that they could not be defeated.

Guilford and Brattleboro were the last battles between the Yorkers and the Green Mountain Boys, and Ethan was glad. He was tired, and his health had been ruined by his long years in prison. In 1783, Ethan's wife Mary died, as did one of his daughters. Ethan decided that the time had come for him to settle down and finish his book. This book was the very same one that Ethan

This is a portrait of Governor George Clinton, who was the first governor of New York State. He served from 1777 to 1795 and again from 1801 to 1804. He fought hard against the settlers of the New Hampshire Grants but never could organize an effective armed resistance to Allen and his Green Mountain Boys.

The full title of Ethan's book is: Reason The Only Oracle of Man, or a Compendious System of Natural Religion. Alternately Adorned with Confutations of a variety of Doctrines incompatible to it; Deduced from the most exalted Ideas which we are able to form of the Divine and Human Characters, and from the Universe in general. *No wonder everyone called the book simply Ethan's Bible!*

and Dr. Thomas Young began together in Salisbury, Connecticut, so many years ago. When Thomas Young died, Ethan got the manuscript from Young's widow. Now he set himself to the task of finishing the work. The book was called *Reason The Only Oracle of Man*, although Ethan's friends called it merely "Ethan's Bible." It was a book about religion, or rather one expressing views against traditional religion. Ethan did not believe in many of the rules and ideas of religion that were followed at that time. He believed that God was a God of nature, and that people should not have to go to church or listen to preachers give sermons. Ethan's book was not well

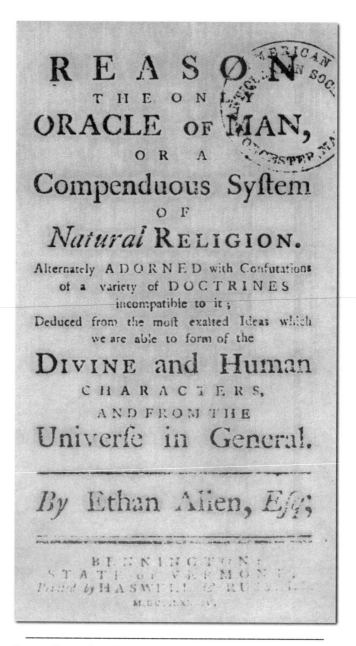

In Ethan Allen's book on religion and philosophy, he argued that commonly held views about God were wrong. This would earn him many enemies in the church, which held great power in Allen's time. Above is the title page to *Reason The Only Oracle of Man*.

Ethan's religious beliefs fell under a branch of religious study known as Deism. Deism holds that God is everywhere in nature, and not outside the world at all. Deism was an idea that was first widely promoted by a group of English writers in the first half of the seventeenth century. Deism spread as it increasingly became a way of criticizing more orthodox Christian religions. By the end of the eighteenth century, it would become the dominant religious attitude among English, French, and German intellectuals and many upper-class Americans. In fact, the first three presidents in the United States all were believers in Deism. It is still a popular school of thought, but during Ethan's time, these ideas were very new and frightening to many people. Reason The Only Oracle of Man got Ethan *in a lot of trouble. Preachers spoke against him in their churches, and booksellers burned their copies of the books. The president of Yale College called Ethan's book "crude and vulgar." All this fuss made Ethan very happy. There was nothing he liked more than stirring up a big mess, and he was very proud of his "Bible."*

received. It was considered so blasphemous that he could not even get it published until 1784. Ethan considered his "Bible" his life's work, even though every preacher in the Union called it evil and dangerous.

The Revolutionary War ended in 1783 with the Treaty of Paris. Vermont remained outside the Union of American States, as its own country with its own laws and government. Vermont even had two newspapers, the *Vermont Gazette* and *The Journal*. At the top of the front page of the *Gazette* ran the words: "With generous freedom for our constant guide/We scorn control and print for every side." Vermonters still wanted to be a part of the Union, however, even though Ethan had become fed up with Congress and grumbled that he would just as soon stay independent. At any rate, the crisis was almost over. There was peace in the Union, and it seemed only a matter of time before New York gave up its territory in the Grants and Vermont could finally become a state.

10. Ethan Settles Down

In 1784, a young woman named Francis Montessori Buchanan moved to Westminster, Vermont, with her mother. Ethan Allen was also in Westminster that winter, finishing up some business in the courts. Soon enough, the townspeople noticed that the young widow and Ethan were spending an awful lot of time together. They were an odd pair. Francis, at twenty-four, was twenty-two years younger than Ethan was. She was the daughter of a Frenchman, and the stepdaughter of a Yorker lawyer who, until his death some years earlier, had hated Ethan Allen. Her husband had been a British soldier who was killed in the Revolution. Nonetheless, Fanny was also well-spoken, funny, and very smart. On the morning of February 9, 1784, Ethan went to the boardinghouse where Fanny and her mother lived. Finding her in the living room, he said to her, "Fanny, if we are to be married, now is the time, for I am on my way to Sunderland."

"Very well," said Fanny calmly, "but give me time to put on my Joseph," a kind of coat. It is thought that

This map shows Sunderland, Vermont, highlighted in orange. Ethan Allen would take his new wife, Fanny, to this town and raise a family.

Ethan and Fanny were extremely happy with each other. Ethan gave his bride a copy of his book Reason The Only Oracle of Man. *On the inside cover, he wrote: "Dear Fanny wise, the beautiful and young/The partner of my joys, my dearest self/My love, pride of my life."*

Ethan may have proposed at an earlier date but the date itself was decided in this spontaneous exchange. Fanny and Ethan went to another sitting room in the house, where the owner of the house was having breakfast with some judges. "Judge Robinson," boomed Ethan, stepping into the room, "this young woman and myself have concluded to marry each other, and to have you perform the ceremony." When the startled judge asked Ethan when he wanted to get married, Ethan impatiently told him, "Now!" The judge began to marry Ethan and Fanny, and everything went well until the judge mentioned God in the wedding vows.

"Hold on, hold on!" Ethan said. "Which God are you talking about? If you mean the laws of God as written in the great book of Nature, pray go on. My team is at the door." The judge sighed and changed the wording to say Nature instead of God. Then Ethan and his new bride jumped in the sleigh that waited at the door for them and sped to Sunderland. Nine months later, Fanny gave birth to a son, Hannibal Montressor Allen.

The next few years were quiet for Ethan and for Vermont. In 1787, there was a rebellion of farmers against the government of Massachusetts, known as Shays's Rebellion. The leader of this rebellion invited Ethan to come and lead them in their battle. He told Ethan that he could be the king of Massachusetts if he would help them. Ethan, however, was happily married and now had two small babies. He no longer wanted to race through the woods on wolf hunts. The Vermonters sheltered Shaysites, as the rebelling farmers were called, in their homes, but they did not join in the revolution in Massachusetts. In fact, Thomas Chittenden and the Allen brothers publicly denounced Shays's Rebellion. They did this to side with Congress. Vermont was still trying to get on the good side of Congress and get into the Union. Unfortunately, Vermont's support for Congress during Shays's Rebellion still did not get them accepted into the United States.

In 1787, Ethan moved with his family to a farm north of the town of Burlington, Vermont. The 350

This is an undated engraving of Daniel Shays's rebel army.
Shays's Rebellion was an uprising of farmers who were
angry over high taxes. These farmers closed courts across
Massachusetts to keep them from taking away their farms.
They were eventually defeated by federal forces, but Daniel Shays,
the leader of the rebellion, was protected when he fled to Vermont.

acres (142 ha) of land overlooked the Onion River, now known as the Winooski River. It was beautiful land, some of the best in Vermont, and Ethan was extremely happy there. He was only forty-nine years old, but his health was failing him quickly. It was time to gather his family about him and relax for a while. He made peace with Levi, and Ira settled just across the river from him. Thomas Chittenden lived in nearby Williston, and two Allen cousins, Caleb and Ebeneezer, settled nearby in South Hero. Ira was still very busy with plans for both Vermont and the Allens, but Ethan was content to farm, write, and spend time with his family.

In Ethan Allen's later years, he lived a much calmer and less rowdy life. Above is an image of Allen's farmhouse, where he settled with his second wife and was surrounded by friends and family.

The winter of 1788 to 1789 was a hard one. There were early frosts followed by months of bitter winter weather. Ethan ran out of hay for his livestock, so he and a hired hand took a sled across the frozen lake to Ebeneezer Allen's home to borrow hay. Ebeneezer put out the word that Ethan was coming. By the time he got there, every Green Mountain Boy in the area had gathered at Ebeneezer's house to greet him. They stayed up all night, drinking and telling stories of wolf hunts and wild adventures in the woods of Vermont. Oddly enough, Ethan was one of the first to fall asleep, and he had to be put to bed by his friends. This was not the Ethan of old who was usually the last man standing at any party. In the morning, though, he was up and about, shouting and waking the men who had fallen asleep on chairs and under tables in the early morning. Ethan and the hired hand got their hay and started back on the long route home. They stopped a few times at houses of people whom Ethan knew, and each time there was drinking to be done and stories to be told. When they were almost home, stories say that Ethan suddenly fell out of the sleigh and landed on the ice. He might have had too much to drink, he might have fallen asleep, or he might have suffered a stroke. Whatever the cause, the giant of the Grants closed his eyes out there on the frozen lake, and he never opened them again. The hired hand got the unconscious Ethan back onto the sleigh and took him home as quickly as he could. He and Fanny put Ethan to bed and called the doctor, but there was nothing to be done for Ethan Allen. He died the next morning, February 12, 1789, at the age of fifty-one. The man who had given his entire life to his beloved Vermont was gone.

On February 16, hundreds of people gathered at Ira Allen's home to see Ethan off. They had traveled from all over the state in a raging blizzard to pay their respects to the man who helped to create Vermont. Ethan had a soldier's funeral, with cannons roaring out over the lake. The Vermont militia fired farewell shots as they lowered Ethan's coffin into the icy ground.

The *Vermont Gazette* published this notice on February 23, 1789:

> *"It is with much regret that we announce the death of General ETHAN ALLEN, who expired in an epileptic fit, on Tuesday last; the patriotism and strong attachment which ever appeared uniform in the breast of this Great Man, was worthy of his exalted character; the public have to lament the loss of a man who has rendered them great service, both in council and in arms; and his family an indulgent friend and tender parent; he has left a most amiable young widow and three small children—and three amiable young daughters by his first wife. While they are deluged in tears for the loss of their best friend, they have the consolation of being left with a handsome fortune."*

This is an image of the Vermont state flag that was adopted after Vermont was granted admission into the United States of America.

Not everyone was sad to see Ethan go. Ezra Stiles, the president of Yale, was one of the people who had been the most offended by Ethan's book. In his journal, Stiles noted that Ethan had died, and added, no doubt with great satisfaction, "And in Hell he lift up his eyes in torment." Ethan probably wouldn't have minded Ezra Stiles's words. In fact, he would probably have enjoyed them.

As for Vermont, Congress finally accepted it into the Union on March 4, 1791. It was too late for Ethan to enjoy his victory, but Thomas Chittenden, Ira Allen, and many other Green Mountain Boys got to witness their little republic being made the fourteenth American state. Ethan had finally won his battle, and he could rest in peace, in the good soil of the state of Vermont.

Timeline

1738	Ethan Allen is born in Litchfield, Connecticut on January 21.
1749	Benning Wentworth, governor of New Hampshire, makes his first land grant, for the town of Bennington.
1755	Joseph Allen dies at the age of 47. Ethan returns home to care for his family.
1762	Ethan Allen marries Mary Brownson.
1764	Britain issues the Royal Proclamation, giving all land west of the Connecticut River to New York.
1770	Ethan Allen arrives in the Grants. On June 28, the Albany Ejection Trials are settled in favor of New York. The Green Mountain Boys are formed at Stephen Fay's Catamount Tavern in Bennington.

1772   Governor Tryon of New York declares Ethan, Robert Cochran, Remember Baker, and five other Green Mountain Boys outlaws and offers a reward for their capture.

1775   On April 19, American patriots and British soldiers fight at Lexington and at Concord, beginning the American Revolution.

On May 10, Ethan and his men invade and take Fort Ticonderoga.

In September, Ethan is defeated and taken prisoner by the British, in whose prisons he will remain for two years and ten months.

1776   A convention of Grants towns meets in Dorset and signs an Association supporting the United States in the revolution against Britain. The Association is signed by Grantsmen, not New Yorkers.

1777   At the Westminster Convention in January, a formal vote for independence is approved. The Grants announces its independence on

	January 17, calling itself "New Connecticut."
	In July, New Connecticut's name is changed to Vermont, and a Constitution is passed.
1778	Ethan Allen is released from a British prison camp in New York.
1783	The Revolutionary War ends with the Treaty of Paris.
1784	Ethan marries Francis Buchanan on February 9.
1787	Shays's Rebellion takes place in Massachusetts.
	Ethan and his family move to Burlington.
1789	Ethan Allen dies on February 12, aged 51.
1791	Vermont is admitted to the Union on March 4, 1791.

Glossary

allegiance (uh-LEE-jence) Support of a country, person, or cause.

appeal (uh-PEEL) An earnest request, or to call upon another for a decision.

blasphemy (BLAS-fuh-mee) The act of insulting or showing a lack of respect for God or religion.

catamount (CAT-uh-mownt) A wild cat.

Committee of Correspondence (kuh-MIH-tee UV kor-eh-SPAHN-dens) A group of leaders in the colonies who began to get together to talk about freedom from England. The committees became the early governing bodies for the colonies as they became states.

Continental Congress (kon-tin-EN-tul KON-gress) A group of leaders from all of the colonies, taken from the committees of correspondence. The first Continental Congress was formed in 1774, to decide whether to form an American Republic.

convention (con-VEN-shun) A formal meeting for a specific purpose.

Deism (DEE-ih-zum) A school of religious thought that denied the role of a creator in nature, or his ability to interfere with the laws of the universe.

denounced (dih-NOWNSD) To have spoken out against, often publicly.

firebrand (FYR-brand) Someone who causes unrest.

furnace (FUR-nes) An enclosed structure in which heat is produced, often for heating a house or melting iron.

Hampshire Grants (HAMP-shir GRANTS) The contested land that lay between New York and New Hampshire in the late 1700s. The name Hampshire Grants referred to grants to the land made by the governor of New Hampshire. The area was known as the Hampshire Grants, or simply the Grants, from roughly 1750 until 1791. Settlers themselves stopped using the term in 1777, when they declared independence and named themselves first New Connecticut and then Vermont.

infidel (IN-fuh-del) Someone who does not believe in a particular religion. Ethan was considered an infidel because of his swearing, using the devil and God's names, as well as his religious beliefs, which were considered wrong and dangerous.

inoculated (in-OCK-yoo-layt-ed) To have been given a small dose of a virus through injection. This weak dose will cause the body to protect itself against the virus in its stronger form.

land-jobbers (LAND-job-erz) People who bought land on speculation, that is, purchased land not to live on, but to resell for a profit.

negotiator (neh-GOH-she-ay-ter) Someone who tries to reach an agreement between different people.

philosopher (fih-LAH-suh-fer) Someone who studies philosophy.

philosophy (fih-LAH-suh-fee) The study of the basic nature of reality, matter, knowledge, and life.

regiment (REH-jih-ment) A grouping of soldiers in an army.

republic (ree-PUB-lik) A country where the power belongs to the people, rather than to a king or a queen.

reputation (rep-yoo-TAY-shun) What most people think of a person or a thing.

Regulars (REG-yoo-lerz) Soldiers in a regular army.

Shays's Rebellion (SHAYS rih-BEL-yun) A rebellion of Massachusetts farmers against the government of Massachusetts in 1787.

spokesman (SPOHKS-man) A person who speaks for a group of people.

stroke (STROHK) A loss of consciousness caused by a rupture of a blood vessel or a blood clot in the brain.

tavern (TA-vern) A bar that serves food and drink.

Tory (TOR-ee) A name for colonists who supported Great Britain during the Revolutionary War.

traitor (TRAY-tor) A person who does something to harm his or her country.

yeoman (YO-man) A person who owns a small farm or plot of land.

Additional Resources

For further information about Ethan Allen, the Green Mountain Boys, or Vermont, check out these books and Web sites.

Books

Cheny, Cora. *Vermont: The State with the Storybook Past*. Shelburne, MA: The New England Press, 1996.

Hahn, Michael T. *Ethan Allen: A Life of Adventure*. Shelburne, MA: The New England Press, 1994.

Web Sites

www.ethanallen.together.com

www.fort-ticonderoga.org

Bibliography

Allen, Ethan. *The Narrative of Colonel Ethan Allen.* Philadelphia: 1779 (Republished by Applewood Books).

Bellesiles, Michael. *Revolutionary Outlaws: Ethan Allen and the Struggle for Independence on the Early American Frontier.* Charlottesville, VA: University Press of Virginia, 1993.

Cheny, Cora. *Vermont: The State with the Storybook Past.* Shelburne, MA: The New England Press, 1996.

Davis, Kenneth. "In the Name of the Great Jehovah and the Continental Congress!" *American Heritage* Vol. XIV, No. 6 (October 1963).

Duffy, John, ed. *Ethan Allen & His Kin: Correspondence 1772–1819.* Hanover & London: University Press of New England, 1998.

Holbrook, Stewart. *Ethan Allen.* Portland, OR: Binford & Mort Publishing, 1988.

Hoyt, Edwin. *The Damndest Yankees: Ethan Allen & His Clan.* Brattleboro, MA: The Stephen Greene Press, 1976.

Krueger, John, ed. *The Best of Ethan Allen.* Benson, VT: Chalidze Publications, 1992.

Linscott, Elisabeth. "Ethan Allen—Soldier, Orator, Author." *The New England Galaxy* Vol. XIX, No. 2 (Fall 1977).

Sabine, David. "Ethan Allen and the Green Mountain Boys." *American History Illustrated* Vol. XI, No. 9 (January 1977).

Index

About the Author

Emily Raabe grew up in Vermont, not far from the Ethan Allen Homestead. She received her B.A. in English literature from Middlebury College and her M.A. in Modern European literature from the University of Sussex in England. She currently lives and writes in New York City.

Credits

Photo Credits

Pp. 4, 70 Courtesy, U.S. Naval Historical Center; pp. 6, 30-31, 71, 83, 92 Courtesy of Map Division, The New York Public Library, Astor, Lenox and Tilden Foundations; pp. 12, 20, 86, 95 © Bettmann/CORBIS; p. 14 As found in the State Archives, Connecticut State Library, Hartford, CT; p. 16 Courtesy, Cornwall Historical Society Photo Collection; p. 18 Courtesy of Norman Sills, Salisbury Association, Inc.; pp. 21, 49, 52-53, 96 © North Wind Picture Archives; pp. 22, 46 © CORBIS; pp. 23, 58 © 1999 CORBIS; p. 24 Courtesy, Emmet Collection, Miriam and Ira D. Wallach Division of Art, Prints, and Photographs, New York Public Library, Astor, Lenox, and Tilden Foundations; p. 33 Image from the Past/Bennington, VT; p. 37 Courtesy of Ms. Holly McKenzie-van Slyck; pp. 40, 62 Special Collections, Bailey-Howe Library, University of Vermont; p. 42 Collections of the Bennington Museum, Bennington, VT; p. 47 © Lee Snider; Lee Snider/CORBIS; p. 51 Courtesy of the Rosen Publishing Group, Inc.; p. 54 Collections of the Geography and Map Division, Library of Congress; p. 61 Picture Library, National Portrait Gallery, London; pp. 64, 76, 77 Courtesy of Vermont Historical Society; p. 66 Courtesy of the Vermont State Archives; p. 72 Washington's May 12, 1778 letter to Congress describing Ethan Allen: Records of the Continental and Confederation Congresses and the Constitutional Convention, Record Group 360; (National Archives Microfilm Publication M247, Roll 168, Item 152, Vol. 6, p. 31); p. 74, 88 Courtesy, General Research Division, New York Public Library, Astor, Lenox, and Tilden Foundations; p. 99 © 1995-2000 Nova Development Corporation.

Series Design
Laura Murawski

Layout Design
Corinne Jacob

Project Editor
Joanne Randolph

BPMS
Media Center